W9-CNO-277

Exploring Infrastructure

BRIDGES

Charlotte Taylor and
Melinda Farbman

Enslow Publishing
101 W. 23rd Street
Suite 240
New York, NY 10011
USA

enslow.com

Published in 2020 by Enslow Publishing, LLC.
101 W. 23rd Street, Suite 240, New York, NY 10011

Library of Congress Cataloging-in-Publication Data

Names: Taylor, Charlotte, author. | Farbman, Melinda, author.
Title: Bridges / Charlotte Taylor and Melinda Farbman.
Description: New York : Enslow Publishing, 2020. | Series: Exploring infrastructure | Audience: Grades 3 to 6. | Includes bibliographical references and index.
Identifiers: LCCN 2018020976| ISBN 9781978503335 (library bound) | ISBN 9781978505070 (pbk.)
Subjects: LCSH: Bridges—Juvenile literature. | CYAC: Bridges. | LCGFT: Instructional and educational works.
Classification: LCC TG148 .T39 2019 | DDC 624.2—dc23
LC record available at https://lccn.loc.gov/2018020976

Printed in the United States of America

Portions of this book originally appeared in *Bridges* by Melinda Farbman.

CONTENTS

INTRODUCTION

The Silver Bridge Disaster

On December 15, 1967, cars and trucks sat in rush hour traffic on the Silver Bridge. The bridge connected Point Pleasant, West Virginia and Gallipolis, Ohio. It crossed over the Ohio River.

Suddenly, there was a loud sound. Some people said it sounded like a gunshot. The bridge shook. Then it collapsed. More than thirty vehicles went crashing into the cold river. It all happened in about twenty seconds.

When people in the area saw what had happened, they rushed to help. They tried to rescue people in the water. But for many, it was too late. Forty-six people died that day. Nine others were badly hurt.

Finding Answers

What went wrong with the Silver Bridge? To understand, we must first look at how the bridge was built. The Silver Bridge was a suspension bridge. This means the part that people drive on is

The remains of the Silver Bridge. It collapsed in 1967, sending cars and trucks crashing into the river below.

suspended, or hung by something. It's a very common type of bridge. But this one was made differently. Most suspension bridges used wire cables to hold them up. Not the Silver Bridge. It was held up with chains called eyebar chains. An eyebar is a metal bar with holes ("eyes") at both ends. Eyebar chains were cheaper than wire cables. Two thick, heavy eyebars were joined together to make a chain. This is important. Other bridges used many lighter eyebars instead of two heavy ones. This meant that if there was a problem

In 1928, Charles Vogel was the first person to drive a car across the Silver Bridge. Vehicles weighed much less in the 1920s than they did in the 1960s, when the bridge collapsed.

with one, the others could still hold. The chains were also made of a new kind of steel.

The Silver Bridge had opened in 1928. For almost forty years, there were no problems. Then disaster hit in 1967. Why? Inspectors found that there was a crack in one eyebar when it was made. The crack was only one-tenth of an inch deep. But over the years, the steel wore down and the crack got worse. It finally broke, and the rest of the chain could not hold.

When the bridge was built in the 1920s, people did not know that the steel in the eyebars could corrode, or wear away. The bridge was inspected many times, but no one could see the crack.

There was another problem that led to the collapse. In the 1920s, cars weighed around 1,500 pounds (680 kilograms). By the 1960s, they weighed more than twice that amount. Trucks were even heavier. The old bridge could not handle the weight of the new cars.

Better Bridges

The Silver Bridge collapse was a terrible tragedy. Many lives were changed forever that day. But there were some positive things that happened because of the disaster. Engineers learned from what went wrong. They never wanted this kind of tragedy to happen again. The bridges that were built after this time were safer and stronger than ever. They were inspected and maintained better.

Bridges are amazing examples of engineering. They give people, cars, and trucks a way to cross water, land, and roads. Without bridges, people would need boats to cross rivers. Without bridges, people would have to go around canyons rather than across them.

In this book, you will learn about the history of bridges, types of bridges, how they are built, and who builds them. You will also read more examples of what happens when something goes wrong with bridges. Finally, we'll take a look to the future and see what's in store for the bridges of tomorrow.

Chapter 1

BRIDGES THROUGH TIME

The earliest bridges were not made by humans. They were made by nature. A tree might fall across a stream. A group of hunters looking for food would then use that tree to get to the other side of the stream. Over time, people slowly started to improve on bridges. They began using stone, logs, and dirt. These bridges did not last long, though. Before the days of concrete, a heavy rain could wash a bridge away.

Today, bridges are built with stone, concrete, steel, and other strong materials. These bridges must be able to carry a lot of weight. They must carry heavy cars, trucks, and trains. But thousands of years ago, bridges had more basic purposes. They were used to move people, water, and goods.

Fallen trees across streams were the earliest bridges.

Early Man-made Bridges

Bridges date back to ancient times. In 537 BCE, a Persian king named Cyrus invented the floating bridge. A roadway lay on top of animal skins. The skins were filled with air, and they floated on the water. Another king built a floating military bridge. He tied together two rows of ships. Then, he laid a walkway on top. The bridge was almost a mile (1.6 kilometers) long. It took Persian soldiers seven days and seven nights to cross it. They took it apart behind them to get away from their enemy.

Romans to the Rescue

The Romans were very skilled builders. They are known for their systems of roads, bridges, and aqueducts that still survive today. The Romans made huge advancements in the construction of bridges.

One major factor that made Roman bridges so strong was their materials. The Romans were the first to use concrete. As you may know, concrete is a very hard substance. But the Romans had a secret ingredient: volcanic ash. They mixed minerals along with

The famous Pont du Gard aqueduct in France is an example of a Roman arch bridge.

small particles from volcanos to make their concrete. The volcanic rocks were incredibly strong. Roman bridges were built to last.

Romans also get credit for inventing the arch bridge. The arch design allowed the bridges to be longer and stronger. They built many arch bridges of wood and stone. Some are still standing today. The Romans also invented the cofferdam. This could be used for building a long bridge across a body of water. A cofferdam is an enclosed area used for a short time while building in water. The Romans used it to keep the area dry while pouring in concrete to install supports in the water. It is also used today to protect workers from water and cave-ins.

London Bridge Is Falling Down

In the year 1210, the famous Old London Bridge was completed. It was built over the Thames River in London, England. It was lined with buildings, shops, and even a chapel. People gathered on the bridge to walk, shop, and visit friends. Ships stopped to unload goods from other countries. It was a busy place.

Old London Bridge was built of stone. It took thirty-four years to finish. More than seven thousand people drowned or were killed in other accidents while working on the bridge. Old London Bridge often needed to be fixed. It always seemed to be falling down. New London Bridge was made of concrete. It replaced Old London

Bridge in the 1840s. The old bridge was taken apart and shipped to Arizona in the United States. Today, people travel to see it.

The Iron Bridge

The Coalbrookdale Bridge in England was built in 1779. It is also known as the Iron Bridge. It was the first bridge to be made with cast iron. It weighed 378 tons (343 metric tons)! The arch bridge was made of more iron than was needed. At the time, no one knew how strong iron could be. By the 1800s, people learned that metals are very strong even when a small amount is used.

Covered Bridges

In the 1800s, settlers in America built many bridges from wood. These bridges had covers made from wood. The covers protected the bridge from rain and snow. Many of these covered bridges have been torn down. But in Parke County, Indiana, thirty-two covered bridges still

A Herd on the Bridge

The Brooklyn Bridge was the first bridge to cross the East River in New York City. People were nervous about using it. They were afraid that the bridge might not be strong enough. The famous circus showman P. T. Barnum (of the Barnum & Bailey Circus) had an idea to calm people's fears. He offered to march twenty-one elephants across the Brooklyn Bridge. On May 17, 1884, he did just that. All of the elephants made it across the bridge. The public was reassured that the bridge was safe.

stand. Parke County has more covered bridges than any other place in the world.

The Brooklyn Bridge

The Brooklyn Bridge in New York City was finished in 1883. It links Brooklyn to the island of Manhattan. The Brooklyn Bridge is a steel suspension bridge. It was the first to be built with steel wire instead of iron wire. There are 75,000 steel wires in each cable. There are four cables. Each cable is more than one foot (0.3 meter) thick. The towers of the bridge rock slightly. They move with the weight of traffic. Stays, or wires, fan out from the towers. They reach the roadway in crisscrossing triangles of steel. They hold the bridge steady in heavy winds. A promenade, or walkway, stretches across the bridge. People often walk on the promenade between Manhattan and Brooklyn.

The Golden Gate Bridge

On the West Coast of the United States is another famous suspension bridge. The Golden Gate Bridge was built in 1937. Its orange, rectangular towers are a symbol of San Francisco, California. The Golden Gate was the first bridge to cross a large ocean harbor. Builders pounded piers into deep, open water. San Francisco has many earthquakes. Some earthquakes are so powerful that they can cause the ground to crack and buildings to fall down. To protect

The Brooklyn Bridge connects Brooklyn with Manhattan. It took fourteen years to build, and at least two dozen people died during construction.

the bridge from falling during an earthquake, the bridge foundation was driven 25 feet (7.6 m) into bedrock. The Golden Gate Bridge has lasted through many earthquakes.

Chapter 2

BIG NAMES IN BRIDGES

Over the years, people have made a name for themselves by building bridges. They often had simple beginnings. But they all had an interest in building something big. They saw their opportunity and worked hard. The bridges that they helped build are still an important part of our infrastructure.

Early Bridge Builders

Thomas Telford was born in Scotland in 1757. He taught himself how to build by helping builders and by reading. Telford was a leader in using iron to build bridges. He built the Menai Straits Bridge in Wales. When it was completed in 1826, it was the longest suspension bridge in the world.

Another important bridge builder was George Stephenson. He was born in England in 1781. At first, Stephenson made shoes and

Thomas Telford designed this aqueduct in the United Kingdom in the late 1700s. Many believe it is one of his greatest achievements.

John Roebling designed the Brooklyn Bridge. Sadly, he died right before construction on the bridge began.

repaired railroad engines for a living. At the age of eighteen, he learned to read and write. Stephenson became an important engineer. George and his son, Robert, made strong railroad bridges in the 1800s.

American James Eads was born in 1820. As a young man, he read math and engineering books. He often searched the Mississippi River for treasure from sunken ships. Later, he used what he had learned about the river to build a railroad bridge in Saint Louis, Missouri.

Building the Brooklyn Bridge

John Roebling was born in Germany in 1806. He came to live in America and built a factory in New Jersey. He also built many bridges. In 1867, Roebling had a plan to build the Brooklyn Bridge across the East River in New York City. Many people thought it could not be done. The distance of 1,600 feet (487.7 m) seemed too long. Roebling said it would work. But John Roebling never saw the bridge completed. One day in 1869, a ferryboat crushed his foot into a pier. Roebling died of an infection.

For the next fourteen years, John's son, Washington, helped build the Brooklyn Bridge. Washington Roebling had studied engineering at Rensselaer Institute in Troy, New York. He fought in the Civil War before taking charge of the bridge project. He worked with others in underwater rooms called caissons. Workers entered caissons through underwater stairways called airlocks. Inside the caissons, workers dug mud from the riverbed. As the mud was removed, the caissons sank into deep water. Pressure built up outside. To stop the water pressure from breaking the caissons, workers pumped air into them. The air pressure became higher in the caissons than it was on land.

When a person moves too quickly from high air pressure to low air pressure, nitrogen gas enters the bloodstream. This is called caissons disease, or "the bends." People can become very sick and die. Many workers building the Brooklyn Bridge became sick from the bends. Washington Roebling was one of them. He became so sick that he had to watch the bridge being built from a bedroom window.

Roebling's wife, Emily, helped him. She became assistant engineer on the project. Every day, Emily carried messages from the Roebling house to the workers at the bridge. Her help moved

Antonio da Ponte

Venice, Italy, is covered in water. To get around, people need bridges— lots of bridges. Back in the 1500s, the people of Venice wanted to rebuild the Rialto Bridge. This foot-bridge crossed the Grand Canal. It was at the busy center of the city. Many people offered plans for the new stone bridge—even the famous artist Michelangelo! But they were all rejected. They had all designed bridges with many arches. The arches would be a problem for boats going under the bridge. Finally, Swiss-born Antonio da Ponte designed a different kind of bridge. Two walkways would meet in the middle at a portico. There was no support at the middle of the bridge. His plan was accepted, and the bridge was built.

The people of Venice were upset. How could this bridge possibly last without any support in the middle? They thought it would collapse into the canal. But da Ponte's design worked. Today, the Rialto Bridge still stands. It is the oldest bridge in Venice.

the project along. In 1883, the Brooklyn Bridge finally opened with fireworks and a parade.

Who Built the Golden Gate Bridge?

Joseph Strauss was a well-known bridge builder in the early 1900s. In 1921, he submitted plans for a bridge that would cross the San Francisco Bay. This was a major undertaking. The bridge would be almost 2 miles (3.2 km) long. There would be many challenges, like strong ocean currents (the bay feeds into the Pacific Ocean) and frequent high winds. But the project was approved. Strauss was hired as the chief engineer.

Construction began in 1933 and took four long years. It was complicated and dangerous work. Strauss put important new safety measures into place, like hard hats, goggles, and a safety net that saved many lives. Finally, in 1937, the bridge was completed. At the time, it was the longest suspension bridge in the world. The people of San Francisco celebrated Strauss and his amazing achievement.

There is no doubt Strauss played a key role in the design and construction of the Golden Gate Bridge. But there was one important person who did not receive credit for his part. Charles Ellis was hired as the design engineer for the bridge. He is reported to have spent seventy hours a week for three years straight working on his designs. But Strauss and Ellis argued at the start of the project, and Strauss fired Ellis. Still,

Joseph Strauss (*right*) stands on the Golden Gate Bridge in 1936 as it is being built. The man on the left is Clifford Paine, who helped design and build the bridge.

it was Ellis's plans, for the most part, that were used in the construction of the bridge. When it was complete, there was no mention of Ellis in any paperwork. Finally, in 2007, seventy years after his death, Ellis was officially recognized for his contributions to the iconic bridge.

Chapter 3

BRIDGE DESIGN

When engineers plan on building a new bridge, they must consider a lot of factors. They must think about the bridge's use. Is it for heavy vehicles? Is it for pedestrians? Does it go over water? How long does it have to be? Does the area get severe weather, like tornadoes, hurricanes, or earthquakes? These events can damage or even destroy bridges.

There are many questions that need to be answered. Then the planning can begin. And one of the first decisions that needs to be made is what kind of bridge it will be.

Kinds of Bridges

Through the years, people have planned many different kinds of bridges. They also have tried using different materials. They learned that there are certain basic bridge designs that work best. And there are only a few basic bridge materials. The three main bridge designs are beam, arch, and suspension.

Beam Bridges

A beam bridge is the simplest kind of bridge. The roadway, or deck, rests on two piers, one at each end. The piers support the weight of the bridge. They also support any cars and trucks on the bridge. The weight travels downward. If a beam bridge is too long or holds too much weight, it will sag in the middle and break. Sometimes, supports called trusses are added below the bridge. (Trusses are made of a framework of triangle-shaped metal that makes the

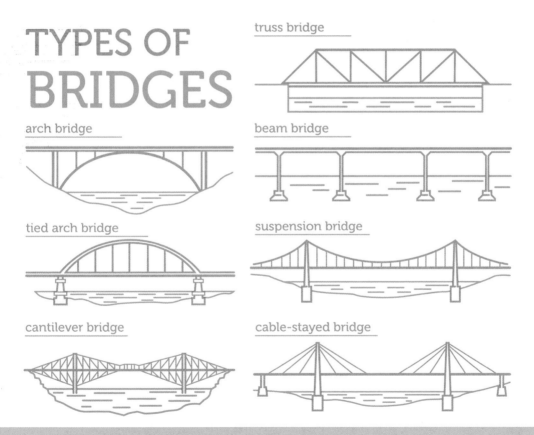

TYPES OF BRIDGES

truss bridge

arch bridge

beam bridge

tied arch bridge

suspension bridge

cantilever bridge

cable-stayed bridge

Bridges can be built in different ways. This image shows some of the main types of bridges. Many of these will be explained in this chapter.

The Winking Eye

Some bridges don't really fit easily into any one category! This is certainly true for the Gateshead Millennium Bridge in Newcastle, England. Also known as the Winking Eye Bridge, it is a pedestrian bridge that crosses the River Tyne. What makes it so unique is that it tilts! It tilts one way to let people walk across. Then, when boats need to go beneath, it tilts up. The bridge got its nickname because it looks like a winking eye when it tilts.

bridge stronger.) Beam bridges can span up to 200 feet (61 m). The span is the distance between two bridge supports.

Some beam bridges can be moved to let ships pass through. One kind of beam bridge can be lifted up in the middle, like draw-bridges. Other kinds of beam bridges are on pivots. They swing sideways to let ships pass.

Arch Bridges

As you learned in chapter one, the Romans designed arch bridges thousands of years ago. An arch bridge is shaped like a half of a circle. This shape makes the bridge strong. The arch is strong because of the way it holds weight. As cars and trucks pass over an arch, weight falls downward. It also falls sideways. The arch catches the weight in many different points along its curve: at the top, along the sides, and at the bottom. As weight spreads sideways and downward, it lessens. Arches can span distances of up to 1,000 ft (305 m).

The tilting Gateshead Millenium Bridge opens
up to let a ship pass underneath.

Suspension Bridges

Suspension bridges are the third main kind of bridge. Cables,
ropes, or chains are strung through tall towers. They are anchored
at either end. Hanging from those cables are another set of cables
that hold up the deck of the bridge, or the roadway. Suspension
bridges usually have trusses underneath. The trusses help to stop
the bridge from moving side to side. A suspension bridge looks
like a stretched-out "M." It seems to be thin. But it is very strong.
Suspension bridges are used when long distances must be crossed.
Suspension bridges can span 7,000 ft (2,134 m).

There are many varieties of the main types of bridges. A lot of these types of bridges are very widely used. Some of the most common are truss, cantilever, and cable-stayed bridges.

Truss Bridges

A truss bridge is made up of pieces that form triangle shapes. These connected triangles are very strong and allow the bridge to carry a large load. Trusses spread out the weight more evenly than a beam bridge.

Cantilever Bridges

A cantilever bridge is related to a beam bridge. It has a horizontal piece with two vertical pieces on either end. A cantilever is some-thing that sticks out from a support on one end, like a diving board. A cantilever bridge is also supported on just one end. The cantilever

The Forth Bridge in Scotland is an example of a cantilever bridge. It was voted the country's greatest man-made wonder in 2016.

stretches out from the vertical support and meets the other canti-lever, which is supported from the other side. This design allows for longer bridges.

Cable-Stayed Bridges

A cable-stayed bridge is similar to a suspension bridge. It has tow-ers and cables that hold up the main span. But unlike the suspen-sion bridge, the cables go from the towers and attach directly to the roadway. There is no need for anchoring them at either end of the bridge. This type of bridge is faster and easier to build than a suspension bridge. It also uses less steel.

Bridge Materials

The basic bridge materials are wood, iron, steel, and concrete. Wood was used in the early days because it was easy to find. But wood is not very strong. It bends easily under weight. Wood also rots over time, and it can catch on fire. Iron is stronger than wood. Steel is even stronger than iron. It is often used for long bridges. Concrete is made of cement, sand, gravel, and water. When con-crete hardens, it is hard as rock.

Metal is added to concrete to make it stronger. Strength is important because a bridge has to hold a lot of weight. The weight of traffic mov-ing over a bridge is called live load. Wind, water, heat, and earthquakes are called environmental load. The weight of the bridge itself is called dead load. People think a lot about load when they design bridges.

Chapter 4

CAREERS IN BUILDING BRIDGES

t takes a whole team of experts to design and build a bridge. Building a bridge requires lots of physical labor. It also requires people with advanced degrees and very specific knowledge. From construction workers to mathematicians and structural engineers, everyone involved in building bridges is an important part of the process.

Education and Building Bridges

Before a bridge can begin to be built, a lot of work and planning must be done. Some workers make measurements. They collect information about the number of cars and trucks that cross a bridge each day. This helps to determine the average stress on the bridge. Calculus is the area of math that explains how quantities,

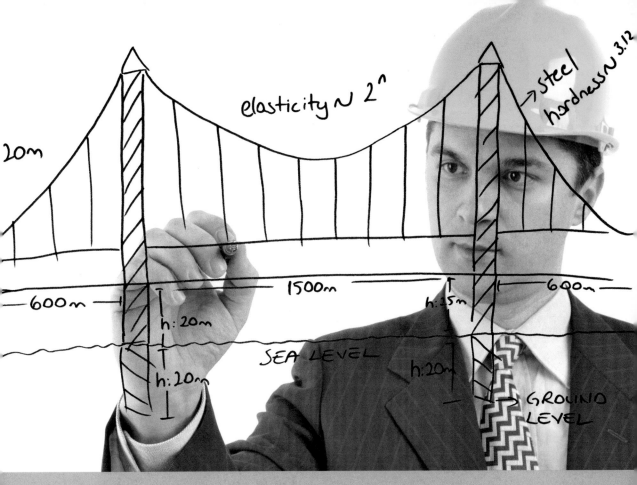

elasticity ~ $2^\wedge$

steel hardness ~ 3.12

20m

600m

1500m

600m

h: 20m

h: 15m

h: 20m

SEA LEVEL

h: 20m

GROUND LEVEL

An engineer must plan out all of the details of a
bridge before construction can begin.

or amounts, are always changing. Workers use calculus to find the
speed of wind at the place where a bridge might be built. They also
use calculus to figure out other forces of nature. Taking all these
kinds of measurements help workers figure out how strong the
bridge needs to be.

Other workers figure out which materials to use to build a bridge.
Workers study chemistry to find out what materials are made of
and how they react to air, water, and heat.

Artists Wanted

People who build bridges must be good at math and science. But what about art? A background in art may not be required, but it could help! A bridge must be safe and functional. But some bridges go well beyond function. Some are considered works of art. The Golden Gate Bridge in San Francisco has an Art Deco influence. The Nescio Bridge in the Netherlands is ultra modern, with sleek lines. On the other hand, the Charles Bridge in Prague is decorated with dozens of statues. Each of these bridges was designed with a certain artistic vision.

Engineers are usually in charge of the project, but architects may also be on the team. Architects may design the structure and determine what it will look like. Then engineers will ensure that it is stable by making the correct measurements.

Physics is the science that includes the study of motion, light, heat, sound, electricity, and force. Structural engineers study physics to find out how structures move.

Other workers study hydraulics, or the force of water. They need to know how water will affect the bridge supports. They also need to understand how the force of water can change over time.

Some bridge workers know about soil and rocks. They learn that different kinds of soils can take greater weights. This information helps workers figure out where and how bridge supports should be built. Other workers make rules about how wide the lanes

Construction workers help move part of a bridge span into place.

should be and about speed limits. They must apply these rules to the design of the bridge.

Some workers are managers. They make sure every step of the project goes well. Others study new materials and designs. They hope to one day improve on what is already known about building bridges.

Building bridges requires a strong math and science background. People who build bridges study structural and civil engineering in college. They must get at least four years of education. Many go on to learn even more. Engineers must pass licensing tests before they can work.

Get Ready to Build

In the past, most engineers were men. But that is changing. Today, more and more women are becoming engineers. People want to become engineers because it lets them use their math and science skills. It also gives people a chance to build something beautiful and important. People who work well in teams are needed as engineers. Those with strong computer skills are also needed.

Young people who want to be engineers can get ready by playing with building toys. They can ask engineers questions about the work they do. They can ask math and science teachers to give them problems that have to do with engineering.

The future of engineering is open to anyone who wants to study math and science, use computers, and work with a team to plan and build structures.

Chapter 5

BRIDGE FAILURES

Bridge accidents are rare. Today, we have strict rules for how bridges are built and maintained. All of the people you read about in chapter four work very hard to make sure that bridges are safe. Still, accidents do sometimes happen.

In the introduction to this book, you read about the Silver Bridge disaster. That bridge collapse was caused mainly by a damaged piece of chain. But there were other factors as well. The bridge was not designed to hold the weight of the vehicles that were crossing it in the 1960s. When a bridge's design is faulty, it can have tragic results. The results can be damage to the bridge, vehicles, or at worst, human life.

Galloping Gertie

The Tacoma Narrows Bridge was built in 1940. It crossed a river in Bremerton, Washington. The bridge was about a mile long. At the time, it was the third longest bridge of its kind in the world. People

The Tacoma Narrows Bridge collapsed in high winds in 1940. Poor planning was blamed for the accident.

planned the bridge carefully. They made the bridge so it would move with the wind. But the bridge moved too much. It twisted and turned most of the time. People saw the bridge twist and turn even before it was done. They called the bridge "Galloping Gertie." The bridge was finished in the late summer of 1940.

A few months later, on the morning of November 7, 1940, the wind was blowing. The bridge began to move. It twisted and turned for almost an hour. Finally, a support cable snapped. The Tacoma Narrows Bridge collapsed. It crashed into the river. A dog was killed but no people were hurt. People tried to find out why the bridge fell down. The disaster taught engineers a lot about planning bridges. They learned that many different things can happen when building a bridge.

In 1951, a new Tacoma Narrows Bridge opened where the old bridge once stood. Many cars and trucks go across this bridge. In fact, in 2007, a second bridge was built right next to the one built in 1951. One bridge carries traffic heading east, and the other carries traffic heading west.

Earthquake Risks

In 1994, an earthquake hit California. Several highway bridges fell down. Many people were killed and hurt. Millions of dollars were used to build new bridges. Engineers had to design these bridges differently. They had to consider something called seismic load. How much force would an earthquake place on the bridge? How could they build the bridge to withstand it?

Today's bridges are stronger and have more advanced materials. They are made to hopefully hold up during an earthquake or other catastrophe. But until the next earthquake, no one knows for sure if these bridges will stay standing.

A new pedestrian bridge in Miami, Florida, collapsed onto a busy highway, killing six people.

Tragedy in Miami

In March of 2018, a new pedestrian walkway was being built at Florida International University in Miami. It crossed a major highway. The walkway would make it safer and easier for students to cross the busy street. On March 15, a few days after the main span was put in place, disaster struck. The bridge collapsed. Cars that had been underneath it were crushed. Six people were killed.

Inspectors immediately started looking for answers. They looked at how the bridge was designed. It had been a new kind of bridge. It used "accelerated bridge construction." This meant that the parts were made in a factory and then moved and put together. There was a report that some of the cables on the bridge were loose. Construction workers were tightening them when the accident occurred. Also, just a few days before the accident, cracks were found in one of the truss supports holding up the bridge. The investigation would take a long time. Most likely, there would be more than one reason for the disaster. It was another example of the importance of caution at every step of the way in bridge construction.

Chapter 6

LOOKING AHEAD: BRIDGES OF TOMORROW

Bridges have come a long way since early man crossed a stream on a log. With today's technology, bridges are safer and stronger than ever before. They are also longer! Some bridges are many miles long. Let's take a look at a few examples of these modern marvels. Then we'll take a peek at what is in store for the bridges of tomorrow.

Akashi Kaikyo Bridge

The Akashi Kaikyo Bridge in Japan may very well be what bridges in the future will look like. It is the longest suspension bridge in the world. It is over 2 miles (3.2 kilometers) long. It is strong enough to

The Akashi Kaikyo Bridge is the world's longest
suspension bridge. It cost almost $10 billion to build.

stand up to Japan's heavy rains and earthquakes. Engineers spent twenty years testing plans. Then, they spent ten years building it. The bridge was finished in 1998.

Danyang-Kunshan Grand Bridge

The Danyang-Kunshan Grand Bridge in China was built for high-speed rail travel. It was completed in 2010 and opened in 2011. In all, the bridge covers a whopping 102.4 miles (164.8 km)! It took about four years to build, which is not long considering the size of the bridge. Bullet trains can speed up to 200 mph (320 kph) as they pass over canals, rice paddies, rivers, and lakes.

Oresund Bridge

The Oresund Bridge connects the countries of Denmark and Sweden. It was finished in July 2000. It is made of concrete and steel. Cars travel on four lanes on the upper deck, or road-way. Trains travel on two tracks on the lower deck. It is the lon-gest combined road and rail bridge in Europe. In total it spans 7.5 miles (12 km) and stretches from Copenhagen, Denmark, to Malmö, Sweden.

What's Trending

Beyond the biggest, longest, or tallest bridges, there are some interesting trends showing up in today's bridges. They may be a sign of what future bridges will look like.

Weather Resistance

You may have seen road signs warning that bridges freeze faster than roadways. One group of Swedish architects found a solution to that problem. The Tullhus Bridge, built for pedestrians and cyclists, circulates hot air. This prevents ice and snow from piling up on it. Other places have also started to use methods to prevent bridges from icing.

Accessibility

More bridges are being built that give pedestrians and cyclists their own space. This is especially appealing for cities with large numbers of commuters. Cycle Snake in Copenhagen, Denmark, is an example of a bridge that was

Floating Along

One of today's most unique bridges is unlike any other you have read about so far. The Governor Albert D. Rosellini Bridge in Washington State is a floating bridge. It crosses Lake Washington, from Seattle to the nearby suburbs. The lake is more than 200 feet (61 m) deep at some points, so a traditional bridge would have been difficult to build.

So how does this floating bridge work? The deck of the bridge sits on top of seventy-seven pontoons. A pontoon is a watertight vessel that floats. In this case, the pontoons are made of concrete (yes, concrete can float!). The four-lane bridge spans 7,710 feet (2,350 m) and is currently the longest floating bridge in the world.

The Kurilpa Bridge in Brisbane, Australia, was made for pedestrians and cyclists. It cost $63 billion to build!

built just for the use of cyclists. With more people looking to limit their driving time, pedestrian and cyclists bridges might be a more common sight in the future.

Going Green

As the world becomes more aware of climate change and global warming, there is a greater interest in the environment in all areas. This includes bridges! Going green may mean including parks or gardens in a bridge's design. It could mean using solar panels for lighting, like the Kurilpa Bridge in Brisbane, Australia. Or it could be even more ambitious. One group of British architects proposed a redesign of the London Bridge. Their plan for the bridge includes rainwater collection, organic food markets, and a wind turbine.

Bridges give us a way to get from one point to another. But they are also much more. Over the years, they have become marvels of engineering and technology. Some are even works of art. Certainly, in the future, bridges will continue to amaze us as they improve the quality of our lives.

CHRONOLOGY

537 BCE Persian king Cyrus invents the floating bridge.

300 BCE – 300 CE Romans invent the cofferdam.

1210 First London Bridge is finished.

1779 Coalbrookdale Bridge is the first cast-iron arch bridge.

1874 James Eads builds the first steel bridge in St. Louis, Missouri.

1883 Brooklyn Bridge opens.

1937 Golden Gate Bridge in San Francisco, California, is the first bridge to cross a large ocean harbor.

1940 The Tacoma Narrows Bridge in Washington collapses due to high winds.

1967 The Silver Bridge, connecting West Virginia and Ohio, collapses.

1998 Akashi Kaikyo Bridge in Japan is the longest suspension bridge.

2000 Oresund Bridge connects Denmark and Sweden.

2011 Danyang-Kunshan Grand Bridge opens in China. It is the longest bridge in the world.

2016 Governor Albert D. Rosellini Bridge opens in Seattle, Washington. It is the longest floating bridge in the world.

2018 Pedestrian bridge at Florida International University collapses.

GLOSSARY

aqueduct A structure that carries water across a distance.

arch A curved structure used as a support over an open space.

beam A long, thick piece of wood, metal, or stone used in building.

bedrock Solid rock under the soil.

cable A thick, heavy rope made of wire.

cantilever A beam that goes past its support.

chemistry The science that deals with substances, what they are made of, what characteristics they have, and how they interact, combine, and change.

earthquake A shaking or trembling of the ground. An earthquake is caused by rock, lava, or hot gases moving deep inside the earth.

engineer A person who designs and builds structures like bridges and buildings.

engineering The work that uses scientific knowledge for practical things, such as building bridges and dams.

physics The science that deals with matter and energy and the laws governing them.

pier A strong structure supporting the spans of a bridge.

span The part of a bridge that is between two supports.

suspension bridge A bridge suspended by cables anchored at both ends and supported by towers.

truss A framework of triangle-shaped metal.

LEARN MORE

Books

Hoena, Blake. *Building the Golden Gate Bridge: An Interactive Engineering Adventure*. N. Mankato, MN: Capstone Press, 2014.

Marsico, Katie. *Bridges*. New York, NY: Scholastic, 2016.

Stine, Megan. *Where Is the Brooklyn Bridge?* New York, NY: Penguin, 2016.

Swanson, Jennifer. *Bridges! With 25 Science Projects for Kids*. White River Jct., VT: Nomad Press, 2018.

Websites

The Great Buildings Online: Brooklyn Bridge

www.greatbuildings.com/buildings/Brooklyn_Bridge.html
Get some quick facts about the Brooklyn Bridge. Search for other bridges and the people who built them.

How Stuff Works: How Bridges Work

www.howstuffworks.com/bridge.htm
Explains the different types of bridges and how they are built.

NOVA Online: Super Bridge

www.pbs.org/wgbh/nova/bridge
Click on "Build a Bridge" to figure out which type of bridge goes where.

INDEX